Bog Arabic

Bog Arabic

Bernadette McCarthy

SOUTHWORD*editions*

First published in 2018
by Southword Editions
The Munster Literature Centre
Frank O'Connor House, 84 Douglas Street
Cork, Ireland

Set in Centaur 12pt
Printed by City Print, Cork, Ireland

ISBN 978-1-905002-55-9

ACKNOWLEDGEMENTS

Thanks to the editors of the periodicals in which some of these poems first appeared: *Agenda, Causeway/Cabhsair, Crannóg, The Irish Examiner, The Linnet's Wings, The Penny Dreadful;* and in the anthology *On the Banks: Cork City in Poems and Songs* (Collins Press, 2016)
Thanks to my husband Joseph Flahive, and my parents Jerry and Helena McCarthy, for their support. I am also grateful to Marc O'Connell, Paul Casey, and Afric McGlinchey for their advice, and to Gill Boazman, Michael Galvin, and Eiman and Asma Mohamed for encouraging my writing.

Contents

In memory of Alexis Landry (1978-2008)

Bog Arabic

It cuts me and it cures me,
the Arabic of my fathers
as the calamus bows to the djinn
of the breezheen
to rise again and dip into the ink
of haggard, ditch, and dyke.

Strangers call it babble,
the Arabic of my fathers,
idioms left rust
in a gap like a turnip-machine,
and on a gate-pier to nowhere
a quartz stone sits like cream
straight off the top of my father's rhetoric:
Bíonn adharca móra ar na buaibh thar lear

another gearagh lost,
another gearagh drowned

Yeosh, yeosh

Culture Café

You could love the teutonic fury
of his Parnell beard, palatine brow,
but when the mouth speaks
it is with a strange froth
that washes away your right to inheritance
in global English white as a Starbucks' mug.

Force the fundamentals
through your enmeshed tongue—
missile strikes, breached charters—
but you will fail to infiltrate his plane;
only drown in disambiguation
as spent hands leave the infant slip
into the iced-latté sea.

COMMONAGE

The rustling map seemed sure
that the railway led to the churches
but the black peat had taken it for its own,
ironing out the seams for bog ore.

So, harmless in our skirts,
we chose a metalled track
that canted us into the sun
as we entered a piebald world

with a pony at every turn;
companionable mares
hung heads over drystone walls
while colts stood tethered,

eyes averted. Stacks of turf rose
but did not hide the flash
of caravans; crude as pig iron,
white as blistering skin.

And yet we strolled on,
loving ponies; yours a well-heeled dun,
mine seeped scraps of brass
from a sorry face.

We met them then against the sun.
One rangy, leaning on a *sleán*,
Lugh in his golden head,
long arms to wield the spade;

the other bulking bronze
in his vest, whose terrier
trotted up, a Belfast sink
slabbering my hand.

The tall one did the talking,
directing us through gates,
while the other, muzzled,
teased the rosary round his neck.

Later in the pub amidst toby-jugs
and knickknacks, we praised
the churches, then the ponies,
but the shared ground was cut

and one man spoke up
as the crowd went dead.
'Stay away from them ponies,
they're a common breed,' he said.

Agoraphobia

It's here again: the soft, dank fear of mouse
as hell is glimpsed in the horizon
of a timber floor.

Chairs are shoved about,
the runnels blocked and bunged,
the borders of a lifetime disappear;

she seeks hope in shadows,
the kick-pleat of a couch
could be a one-night grace,

but stays put. Press-board snaps. The desk
jerks foot-to-foot, tremor thickens
into terror, she pisses out her quick

then shrieks into the piercing scent of paint:
one blatant sprint into the open grave
as clarity skins her raw from head to tail.

Ghost in the Jack Lynch Tunnel

After 'Ghostly Figure Spotted in Jack Lynch Tunnel', Cork's Red FM News, 3/10/2015.

He wanders the N40 like a migrant,
half-remembering into being his form:
the flat wool cap from Shandon factory,
the jacket bought in Mallow on mart day;
he wills his lungs soft as floss,
palm lines sugar-mice pink, his
gorgeous liver red as a cow-house door
so that he almost scents caviar of horse-dung,
rush of pig's gore. But he cannot
quite recall how life should sound
and the legs come out twisted as a dream;
tweed ends weaving into a white, dividing line
as he cedes to the concrete of the tunnel,
forgetting himself in the rat-black traffic.

Parallel North

The silver trump of freedom had roused my soul to eternal wakefulness.

Frederick Douglass

White stars shoot my eyes in Shannon
as I enter the muzzle of US security;
bare feet, bags, babies in bondage
flow down parallel lines in estuarine terror.
Waiver me, wave me on
across the epoxy floor.

Fred peeped from the closet
as the Captain set to work
on Hester's denigration.
He told her cross her hands
then hooked them to a joist
so she stood contrapposta,
stripped back smooth for the sculptor's
lash, each aphrodisiac scar
a belt of Venus in the making.

I pass into the full-body scanner.
'Raise your arms.' Us Irish were
blacks too, turned inside out,
till we evolved: whiter, triter, richer.
Farmer's tan blanched
by backscattering light,
I soar to paradise in orant praise.

Yasuke was tall and strong. We thought
he was covered in ink. The Lord
ordered him stripped from the waist up
and they scrubbed his skin clean.

He was, in fact, quite black.

SMERWICK

...the Scandinavians used 'butter' as a term of praise for land... smjör-vik is an
Old-Norse realisation. J. Sheehan *et al.* 2001, 'A Viking Age Maritime Haven'.

You stop on the moon-slick sand
and turn to Ballinrannig.
'There's too much light.'
A stone's throw between us
then another, and another
as you skim back the strand
to check the electric blanket.

I stare at the amber smear
of windowpane and wonder
did those women feel the same
stone-slump in the belly
as the butter *vik* was consumed
by a Northern fleet?

A wheyed shade slipshodding
curds up into you.

Ibn Fadlan in Chorasmia

I sleep swaddled in a tent in a house within a house,
raw cheek frozen to the pillow.
The air is gum Arabic
that clings to the soul.

No men here. Only shawlies,
wrapped in furs and skins with
frigid eyes exposed. A pair left

the camp to search for wood
but forgot their flints. They
sheltered by the drift of their dying camels.

No men here but brutes.
Returning from the bath, my beard
was a frozen mass that drooled before the hearth.
I have not seen my reflection in some time.

No mimbar here to mark the hours,
time lurks in the slit of a nib.
My rank hangs delicate
as ice from the horses' tails.

I saw a great tree cleft in two
and the earth torn apart from cold.
We must start west.

Inishkea North

Steatite cuts smooth,
foam-light as brain;
stone to weight the warp
of a pagan loom
damns dog-whelks, whorls,
monkish whirligigs,
skins of clay trod,
lashed to muck, trod
again to the salt-rimed church
where the priest wore a stole
steeped in wine of crushed *purpura,*
linen beneath creamy as the scud
of a long-boat in the bay; he told them
not one grain would go uncounted
by the saviour lanced in stone,
beaming at the brethren
as the spear clenched his choke.

The stone-clad mound
still scurfs new hope:
puffins and wild game,
barley on the machair;
the grinning Christ tramped
into a suet of small
finds and charred oats
till their pots wore through,
the iron wept itself out into pan;
and all that was left
above the ascetic sand
was the scut of a rabbit gouging
out the world's end.

Modern Conversational Arabic

'He is a brother not a father.' Serving
the girls leaf-tea from her thermos,
my Arabic teacher talked about her husband
who was courting high court caliphs
into signing refugees' papers, stringing

their tales from one night to the next.
'A good man.' And without him, syntax snagged,
though between us the ragged ends met:
her bride-price mucking up the Nile callows,
an equation that outwore the cloven years

of asylum; the ministerial handshake,
ached for, yet awkward in the end,
cuffs brushing at a wake. She kittered
an empty cup from my hand, snapped her veil:
'I'm sorry the troubles in the East,'

then took the scrap of chalk again
and pulling back her sleeve blazed us down
the seams of sound succeeding sound, tonguing
tacit vowels into the chastity
of consonants; as algebra binds

the broken parts she wove a universe
into her lace of ligature. *Assalamu alaikum.'*
I knew that the words were backwards,
that a dagger hung over the *alif,*
an assassin could stop my glottis

with the sadist twist of *sad*,
but followed the letters off the page
into her eyes; Donyazad, world-freer,
on the azimuth of her brow, who with
the wisdom of a scripture seemed to say:

'You can burn me but the words will still be spoken;
you can shoot me but my children will live on;
you can scorn me but I am your mother, your daughter,
your father and your brother.'

Artemis in a Bomb-blast

After F.E. McWilliam 1974, 'Woman in a Bomb-blast',
The Crawford Art Gallery, Cork.

Once, she was tripped up on the high street.
Rough lads roared as she thrashed
in the smother of her skirts

and she swore never to be shamed again;
crossing her legs nicely in the Abercorn café,
Artemis cast her gaze upon the crowd

but

the bomb-blast wrapped itself around her,
gel and limb and jag brazing in hate,
her slag run off into the street

till all that seemed to be left
were pranks of thumbs and teeth,
buttons blasted into eyes,

her own eyes into buttons,
and the bold-as-brass taste
of burnt flesh.

Only the sculptor saw and grafted back in place
that final moment of poise when,
elbows arched, sinews drawn,

she turned out her soles, flexed her knees,
and danced against the bomb
in a riot of drapery.

TARTEEL

I am no anthropologist but I know
there is no term in English for *tarteel*;
it does not mean to chant or sing the Book,
just so there is no word for your look
as the verse yearns from your holy throat:
stone-cold dam, impenetrable as cold stone;
dried-up Nile that nourishes yet chokes,
overgenerous in turns, so as to coax
numb earth back to feeling. And I wonder
if they did it even to you, the shutting up
smooth as close of water over stone-skim,
stitching out a stave to sing a bride,
their scissors flashing cleanly as
tarteel: a sound that has no proper name.

On the Probability of Moving to Dublin

I wept. Then went to the city hall to meet the mayor
with my Arabic teacher's husband, who rose
to the occasion of his doric, undoffed hat
as cream-tea pilasters supped
light from the hardwood floor;
his patent leather shoes were polished black
and the tricolour badge on his chest was Cork:
green counsel of bearded butter-roads, glenning into gorse,
the blank of believing in nowhere else, but needing to go,
the gold, dropped eggs in the market, a sob of burst yolk.

THE GREEN FIELDS

'ERC MAQI MAQI-ERCIAS [MU] DOVINI[A]': *Ogham stone,*
Dunmore Head, Dingle, c. 500 AD.

Inaccessible, or so the archaeological inventory states,
locally termed the Green Fields, where Brendan graced
the church before migrating, but too byzantine
in its network of stone walls, too fretted and far
for real Cork scholars to categorise. Undocumented paradise.

And we go because we have to,
forsaking our Golf below Brandon's hem, Kerry colours
flying leeward side. The road soars like a miracle
over native muck and you wonder what snobbery built it;
I tell you pilgrims were easy money

in the prevaricating, pre-modern world:
once up Brandon seven times to Rome, some bishop said.
Holy Marys flash on the uterine horizon,
behind my whites, your hopes. This could be
our epiphany after all. This could be our end.

Crows swarm, starving for the burnished eyes
of sheep. A spoiled cabin preaches from the north.
I could have been a sibyl assaying the glacial entrails
as you smoked pipe in complement to the surging sea,
picking and choosing lice, surveying extremities

of Empire, free to lean over and scratch the belly of Dovinia.
Higher still, where dank cracks smuggle Spanish flora, sky
yields the Green Fields, stark as a satellite
on the madcap cliff-locked coombe 1500 feet below,
and they are inaccessible, their walls blazing

from a beehive heart, slope straining at an impossible outcome,
blind principals of precipice. I can't go forward or back
yet you push on like a Kashmiri lorry,
exalting me though I am unhillworthy.
Salt gasp. Sphagnum slide. Walking on water.

Turns out it is a monastery, millstones and all, where
chosen ones made good ground from Godhead and dung.
Killers came, left. Peasants took asylum.
I lie amongst ticks, trace the love trail of Uí Bhreasail,
until a gull cries: 'The generations poured into each other,

pots and wives portered down
until the spuds slobbered gently into autumn.
Those who did not mushroom back to green
crawled upslope and stowed into a coffin sailing west.
Now there is only this: sky become sea. The vacant lazy beds.'

Hell Ghazal

Your fasting hand upon my knee is hell.
Your hennaed wrists, an augury of hell.

The North Side is a mosque
and all is tessellation as I wend down Fair Hill.

Traffic interweaving, slates overlapping,
bricks rising to a paradise red as hell.

Slippers jilted by the door for a sun
that won't go under. Thirsty as hell.

There is poetry in the fall of your sleeve
as you tattoo me, fringe delicate as a seashell.

Three dates to break the fast. Bowing as you
pour, our new Queen of Cashel.

Kohled brows can never chasten Berber eyes.
Open them wide and punish me to hell!

May Voting 2015

I

The holy Mary font fell from the wall
and cracked in two. Thirty years she'd stretched
her arms over the kitchen door,
but as they set off for the old school,
renewed, smarting pure, she cast
the fullness of her faith at their feet.
'The cord has snapped at last,' Mamie said,
yet he had heard the milk-white shriek.

As the jeep rounded the fairy wood again,
they saw a strange Kilkenny reg, some young
man staring dead ahead, his wife
('or what is she at all?') digging out bluebells.
He slowed, but then pushed on, reluctant to stop,
only knowing that grace had forever been lost.

II

I take out the scones too late,
black as the Gold Blend Adam
stirs again and again. The mad heat's
burnt his neck. 'You vote?'
I gesticulate, grasping the townland,
the world in a Yes! Yes! embrace;
'No vote for Polish men!'
He shoos us, flaxen sahib.
 'Too far east is west,' my mother states.

CAUGHT

In muck and rheum
he stalks safari-backed
through the gap
I'm caught
in the running
of his rose-veal
eye

she should've known
the cows are gone to dairy

frail moan
swells to bellow
as hooves shunt shite
and choler-shot
he charges
at the bait

I am Europa
rutted on a gate

Farewell to Aran

I know you Aran but imperfectly
as clint the gryke, as land the sea,
as a fulmar knows the edges in between
wing and sky

for you twist away from my pilgrim prayers
in a kidney-clutch, yet I can smell
the bronze tang of thyme
that keens your breath

and over your breast into nothingness
the giddy *dún* runs *chevaux de frise*
far from the cursor's blink
at the foot of the page.

I have seen a fish caught in a saxifrage net
at the bed of a holy spring;
through the lace of a drystone gap
I have pulled the Twelve Pins;

I have measured a limestone hut
and reeled off Synge;
but I cannot grasp what lies
beneath the church of the crippled ridge

at the cusp of a crinoid's arm
in the cup of an Aranman's head.

NIGHT VISION

Every night after the strike Hasan
would send himself to Heaven;
he'd shut his supernova eyes, press
his brow against the rug
and burst into a million
liberated moons. He'd rip the bra-strap
off the world, let east go west,
grasp the hot palm of the Pleiades
and stroke the Lion's brow, lead
the Mourning Maidens down
the star-spine. But one night
in the boundless sea of universe
he grew cool as onion-milk, weary
of the light that bombed the Earth.
So he followed the course
of a drone, true as hellfire,
American prick of composite steel
smart to its exact parts,
and shot into the face of the Sun,
blinding God.

Ùig Beach

You offer me whisky for warmth, good Tallisker,
unfold my fold-out throne, then your own,
and bask in your hollow, spreading your legs wide
as Ùig Beach divests itself for plunder.
All this camp is yours, from the showers
to the cunning loins of the dunes
and the fickle sanity of the smiling shore.

Wind brags against sea, skins us raw
into submission as we storm up the beach,
bare feet crushing shells into a morse
known only by gulls and guillemots;
never to be sworn to ivory or metred
on brass strip. Falling upon a cower
of cowelled men from the BBC

bent about a mound fresh-dug as a child's
sandpit, strewn with replica chessmen,
I see the bishop, complacent in the gale,
unreasonably white, untouchable;
the hot-and-bothered queen, palm on cheek
as if struggling to recall
baby babble of a foreign land.

This camper van could be the moulded silence
of a thousand years; here you are brown tusk,
berserker within you grinding down
on guarded patience. Muscles beard
into questions. Razor clams stab the salted flat.
Hoard it all while you can:
this kist won't keep us here forever.

Bog Arabic

Yeosh: said by farmers to soothe a cow when milking her.

Inishkea North

After S. Greene 2009, 'Settlement Identity and Change on the Islands of North-West Mayo' (PhD, UCD).

The Green Fields

or more commonly Fothair na Manach, is a cluster of stone structures north of Mount Brandon, Co. Kerry, that features evidence of early medieval as well as 18th/19th-century settlement. Locals say a Fitzgerald family reoccupied the site due to pressure from landlords.

Ùig Beach

In 1831 a hoard of 12th-century ivory chess-pieces were discovered in a small stone chamber at the edge of Ùig Beach, Lewis, Scotland.